Arkas,
*IT'S ONLY FOREVER*

© Arkas, Greece

Translation: Ingrid Behrmann

«grammata» editions
7, Gravias Str., 106 78 Athens, Greece
tel.: 210-38.07.689 - fax: 210-38.10.892

www.protoporia.gr
www.arkas.gr

# Life HEREAFTER

## by ArkaS

*«grammata»*

# Life HEREAFTER
## by ArKaS

# IT'S ONLY FOREVER

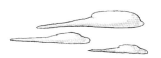

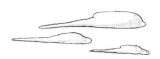

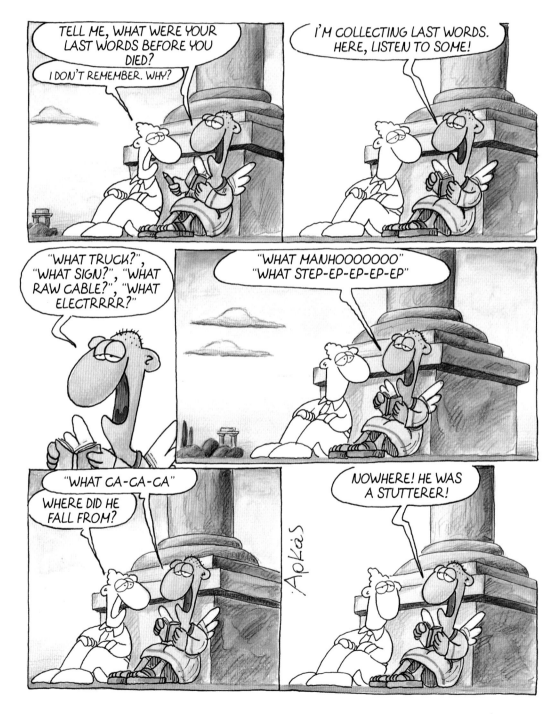

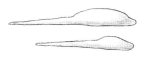

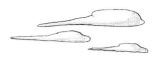

WE MUST BE IN HEAVEN, RIGHT?

SEEMS SO!

...BUT THAT DOESN'T MEAN ANYTHING MUCH BECAUSE AFTER A WEEKEND WITH MY FIVE GRANDCHILDREN ANYWHERE WOULD SEEM LIKE HEAVEN TO ME!

IT'S REALLY STRANGE THOUGH! EVERYTHING LOOKS SO REAL AND YET SO DISTANT!

...AND THEN THERE'S THIS WEIRD SMELL!

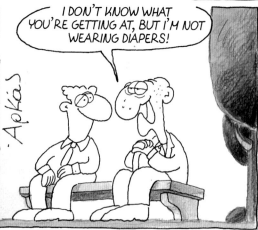

I DON'T KNOW WHAT YOU'RE GETTING AT, BUT I'M NOT WEARING DIAPERS!

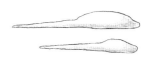

BUT IT'S NOT FAIR THAT EVERYTHING SHOULD END WHEN YOU DIE! WE SHOULD GET A SECOND CHANCE!

STOP WHINING!

WITH DEMOGRAPHIC IN DECLINE YOU SHOULD FEEL LUCKY THAT YOU EVEN HAD A FIRST CHANCE!

HAVE YOU ANY IDEA HOW CROWDED THE UNBORN DEPARTMENT IS? THEY WAIT IN LINE FOR DECADES TO BE BORN!

...AND WHEN THEY FINALLY SUCCEED THEY'RE MOSTLY BORN CHINESE!

Αρκάς

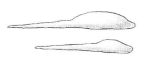

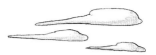

CAN I SIT WITH YOU?

NO! HAS ANYBODY ASKED YOU TO?

WHEN WILL YOU STOP THIS STUPID HABIT OF TURNING UP EVERYWHERE WITHOUT AN INVITATION?

I HATE THE SUICIDES!

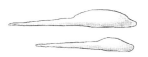

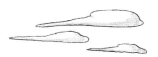

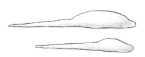

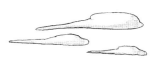

YOU STILL DON'T REMEMBER ME, DOC? I'M THE ONE WITH THE PERFORATED STOMACH WHOM YOU TREATED FOR PILES!
YES... THAT RINGS A BELL!
...ONE OF THE VERY FEW CASES WHERE I A MADE A WRONG DIAGNOSIS!
VERY FEW?! THAT'S A LAUGH! YOU'VE SENT MORE PEOPLE HERE THAN GENGHIS KHAN!
...OF COURSE YOU UNDERSTAND, ANGEL, THAT OVER A LONG CAREER IT IS ONLY HUMAN TO COMMIT ONE OR TWO MISTAKES!
ONE OR TWO?! YOUR MISTAKES HAVE FORMED AN ASSOCIATION OVER HERE!
...WHAT'S IMPORTANT HOWEVER IS THAT I LEARN FROM MY MISTAKES!
THAT'S TRUE! HE LEARNS TO MAKE THEM WITH HIS EYES SHUT!
...THE MISTAKES WE DOCTORS MAKE CAN RARELY BE CORRECTED, SO IMAGINE OUR RESPONSIBILITY! OTHER PEOPLE USE WITE-OUT TO COVER UP THEIR MISTAKES, WHEREAS WE DOCTORS...
...MARBLE!

SO WHO GOVERNS HERE THEN, ANGEL?

MANY! THERE ARE WHOLE HOSTS OF ARCHANGELS, SAINTS, BLESSEDS AND SO ON, MANAGING THE ADMINISTRATION. IT'S A COMPLICATED SYSTEM OF DIRECTIONS, DEPARTMENTS, SUB-DEPARTMENTS, UNITS...

SOUNDS VERY BUREAUCRATIC AND STIFF TO ME... IS IT EFFECTIVE?

EFFECTIVE?! THEY WORK WONDERS!

UNFORTUNATELY I BELONG TO THE LOWEST RANKS. I SHOULD HAVE BEEN MADE ASSISTANT TO A DEPUTY ARCHANGEL BY NOW, BUT THEY'RE KEEPING ME DOWN.

WHY?

I HAVE NO IDEA! IN THE REPORT CARDS IT SAYS THAT I AM NOT WORTHY OF PROMOTION BECAUSE I AM, SO THEY SAY, TOO VAIN AND CONCEITED! ME! VAIN?! I WHO AM SO SIMPLE AND UNPRETENTIOUS THAT I DON'T EVEN WEAR MY HALO!

OH YES, SO I SEE! WHY NOT?

BECAUSE IT DOESN'T SUIT ME AT ALL!

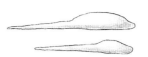

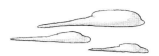

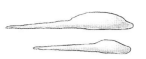

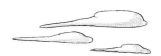

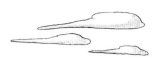

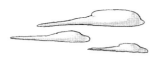